LET'S EXPLORE SCIENCE

Sound & Music

△ David Evans and Claudette Williams □

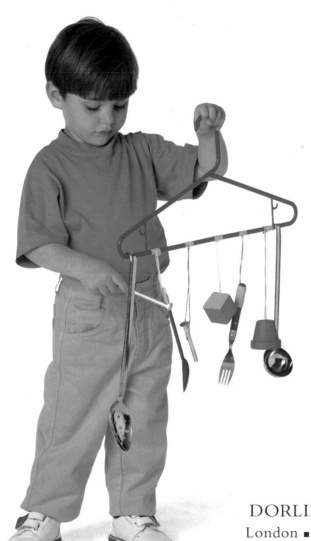

DK

DORLING KINDERSLEY

London ▪ New York ▪ Stuttgart

Note to parents and teachers

Young children are forever asking questions about the things they see, touch, hear, smell, and taste. The **Let's Explore Science** series aims to foster children's natural curiosity and encourages them to use their senses to find out about science. Each book features a variety of experiments based on one topic, which draw on a young child's everyday experiences. By investigating familiar activities, such as bouncing a ball, making cakes, or clapping hands, young children will learn that science plays an important part in the world around them.

Investigative approach

Young children can only begin to understand science if they are stimulated to think and to find out for themselves. For these reasons, an open-ended questioning approach is used in the **Let's Explore Science** books and, wherever possible, results of experiments are not shown. Children are encouraged to make their own scientific discoveries and to interpret them according to their own ideas. This investigative approach to learning makes science exciting and not just about acquiring "facts". This way of learning will assist children in many areas of their education.

Using the books

Before starting an experiment, check the text and pictures to ensure that you have assembled any necessary equipment. Allow children to help in this process and to suggest materials to use. Once ready, it is important to let children decide how to carry out the experiment and what the result means to them. You can help by asking questions, such as "What do you think will happen?" or "What did you do?"

Household equipment

All the experiments can be carried out easily at home. In most cases, inexpensive household objects and materials are used.

Guide to experiments

The *Guide to experiments* on pages 28-29 is intended to help parents, teachers, or helpers using this book with children. It gives an outline of the scientific principles underlying the experiments, includes useful tips for carrying out the activities, suggests alternative equipment to use, and additional activities to try.

Safe experimenting

This symbol appears next to experiments where children may require adult supervision or assistance, for example, when they are heating things or using sharp tools.

About this book

Sound and Music encourages children to make and listen to a range of sounds. They are challenged to create different sounds, first by using their voices and bodies, and then by using instruments, including those that they have made themselves. In carrying out the experiments children will find out that:

- sounds are created by making objects vibrate, for example, when they are plucked, struck, shaken, scraped, or blown;

- the pitch of a sound can be changed by making an object vibrate at a different speed;

- the quality, or timbre, of a sound depends on the material from which the instrument is made and the way it is played;

- the loudness of a sound depends on how hard the instrument is played and how far away the listener is from the sound;

- sound can travel through different materials;

- we hear sounds with our ears and special equipment can help us to hear very soft sounds;

- very loud sounds are unpleasant and should be avoided.

With your help, young children will enjoy exploring the world of science and discover that finding out is fun.

David Evans and Claudette Williams

Can you make sounds?

Can you use your body to make different sounds?

Stamping and clicking
Can you stamp your feet and click your fingers at the same time?

Singing
Can you sing a song? Can you sing it softly?

Shouting
How loudly can you shout to a friend?

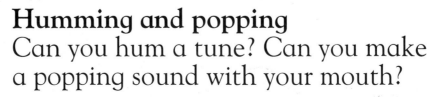

Humming and popping
Can you hum a tune? Can you make a popping sound with your mouth?

10

Whistling

Are you good at whistling? Can you whistle a tune?

Patting

Can you make a sound by patting your leg? Can you make a different sound if you pat your head? Can you do both at the same time?

Clapping

Can you clap hands with a friend? How quickly can you clap? How slowly can you clap?

Do you know a clapping song? Can you clap in time to the song?

Can you twang, pluck, or flap it?

Try these experiments and see if you can make different sounds.

Fork

Can you make a sound by plucking a fork? Now try banging a fork on the floor. Does it make a high or low sound?

Ruler

Hold a ruler on the seat of a chair. Press down one end of the ruler and then let go. Does it make a sound?

Elastic band

Stretch a long elastic band around a chair. Does it make a sound when you pluck it? What happens to the sound when you pull harder?

Cardboard

What sort of sound does cardboard make when you flap it?

If you flap kitchen foil, will it make the same sound?

Box guitar

Can you make a guitar with elastic bands and a box? Use thick and thin bands. Do all the bands make the same sound when you pluck them?

If you use a coin to pluck the guitar, will it sound the same?

Can you tap or bang it?

What different things can you find to tap or bang? Can you make loud and soft sounds? What makes the loudest sound?

Take care when making sounds with glass bottles or jars.

Tapping

Can you make different sounds by tapping? Can you tap with your fingers? Try tapping with different beaters. Do you think a wooden spoon will make the same sound as a metal spoon?

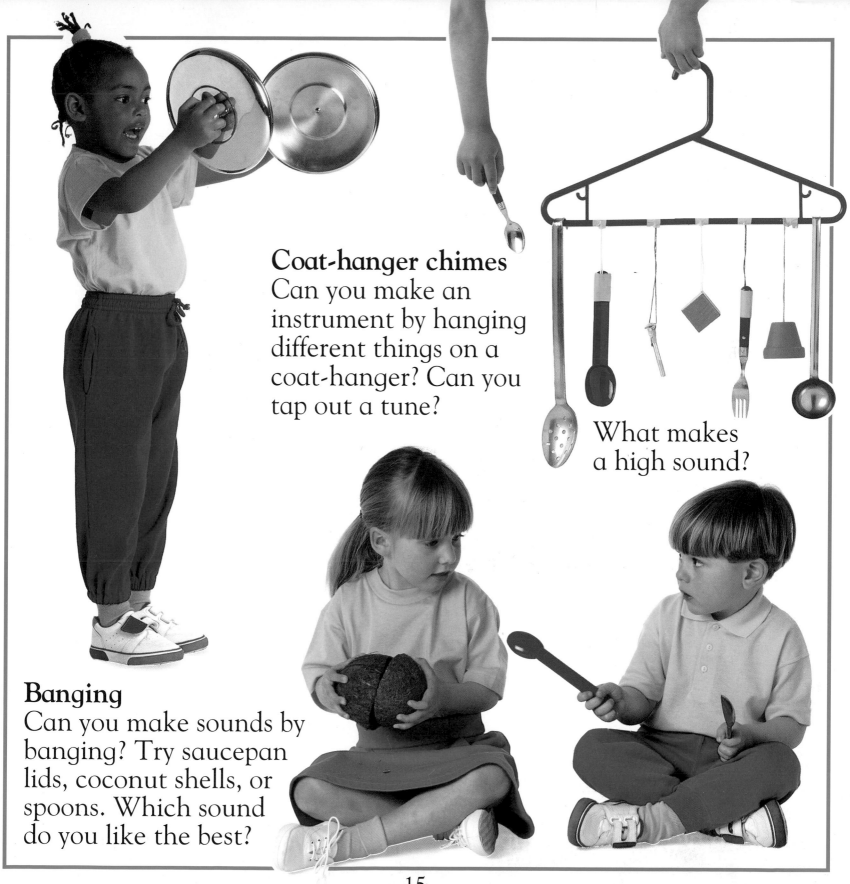

Coat-hanger chimes
Can you make an
instrument by hanging
different things on a
coat-hanger? Can you
tap out a tune?

What makes
a high sound?

Banging
Can you make sounds by
banging? Try saucepan
lids, coconut shells, or
spoons. Which sound
do you like the best?

15

Can you shake or scrape it?

What things can you find to shake or scrape?

Shaking
Can you make some shakers? Find some pots, plastic bottles, cups, and boxes.

Put things such as beads, rice, or corks into your containers. Make lids with plastic film or paper.

Use an elastic band or tape to hold the lids in place. Which shaker makes the best sound?

Rattling

Can you make this shaker? Thread some things on to a length of string. Tape the end of the string to a stick. What happens when you shake the stick?

Will it sound the same if you thread only buttons or bottle tops on to the string?

Scraping

Can you make sounds by scraping? Try running a comb along the edge of a piece of cardboard. Does it make a sound?

Use a spoon to scrape the spiral binding on a notebook.

What happens when you scrape slowly?

Can you blow it?

Can you use air to make different sounds?

Reed-pipe
Make a reed-pipe with a large paper straw. Flatten one end of the straw and cut it to a point. What sort of sound does the straw make when you blow through the pointed end?

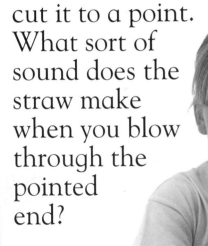

What happens to the sound when you cut the straw in half?

Bottle
Try blowing softly over the neck of some bottles. Does a large bottle make the same sound as a small bottle?

Whistle
How can you make a very loud sound with a whistle?

18

Pan-pipes

Can you make some pan-pipes? Stick some drinking straws on to a piece of tape.

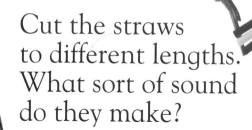

Cut the straws to different lengths. What sort of sound do they make?

Paper bag

Blow up a paper bag. What happens when you burst it? Does the bag make a loud or soft sound?

Balloon

What happens when you slowly let air out of a balloon? Does it make a sound?

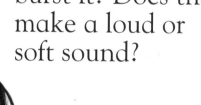

Is the sound loud or soft?

Which things make soft sounds? Which things make loud sounds?

Fizzy drink
What can you hear if you put your ear near a fizzy drink? Can you hear better if you shut your eyes?

Bell
Ring a bell near your ear and then ring it far away from your ear. When does the bell sound louder?

Watch
Does a watch tick loudly or softly?

Cymbal
Can you make a loud sound with a cymbal?

Drum
How can you make a loud sound with a drum?

Listening to sounds

Try listening to different sounds, such as paper rustling, a radio playing, or bells ringing. Ask a friend to make the sounds for you.

Can you stop yourself from hearing the sounds? Try covering your ears with your hands or with some cotton wool. Which works better?

21

Can you hear through things?

Try these experiments to see if you can hear through things.

Floor
What can you hear if you put your ear to the floor?

Balloon
Can you hear a watch ticking through a balloon? What happens if you fill the balloon with water?

String telephone
Ask an adult to help you to make this telephone. Make a hole in two plastic cups. Thread a length of string through the cups. Use two buttons to hold the cups in place at each end of the string.

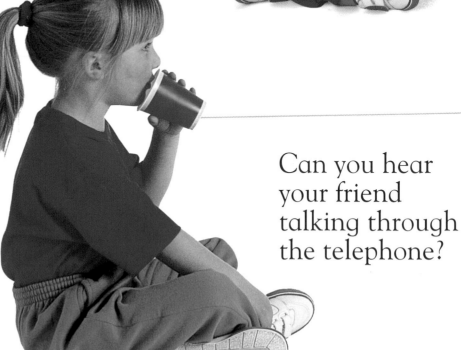

Can you hear your friend talking through the telephone?

Stethoscope
Tape two funnels on to a length of tubing to make a stethoscope. Can you hear a watch ticking through the stethoscope?

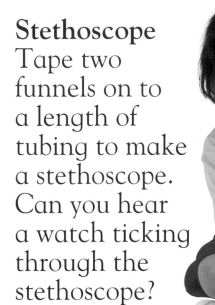

Broom handle
Put a broom handle gently on to a plastic watch. What will happen if you put your ear against the broom handle?

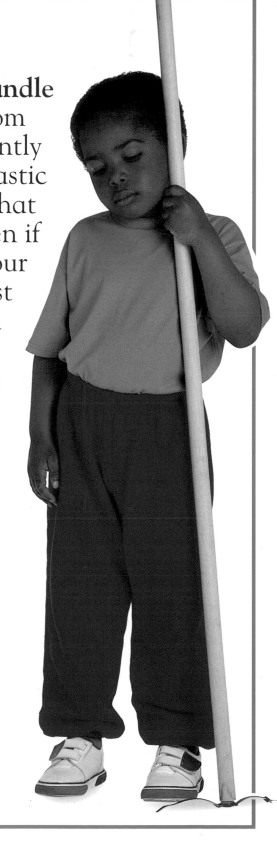

Can you hear round a corner? What happens if the string is slack? What do you think will happen if you use thicker string?

Can you feel it moving?

Try these experiments to find out if things move when they make a sound.

Guitar
What can you feel when you put your finger on a plucked guitar string?

What can you see when you pluck the string?

Neck
Put your fingers on your neck. What can you feel when you talk, sing, or shout loudly?

Cymbal
Ask a friend to strike a cymbal. What can you feel when you put your finger gently on the edge of the cymbal?

Kazoo

Can you make a kazoo with a comb and some tissue paper? Fold the paper around the comb. Put your lips to the paper and hum a tune. How do your lips feel?

Drum

Put some rice on a drum. What do you think will happen when you hit the drum?

Triangle

Tape a piece of thread to a table-tennis ball. What happens when you hold the ball against a triangle just after a friend has struck it?

Can you make music?

Can you form a band with your friends?
What will you play? Who will play first?
How will you know when to end?

Bottle xylophone
Fill some bottles
with different
amounts of water.
Do all the bottles
make the same
sound when you
tap them?

Bucket drum
Can you keep
time with a drum?

Bottle pipes
Can you find a bottle
that makes a low sound?

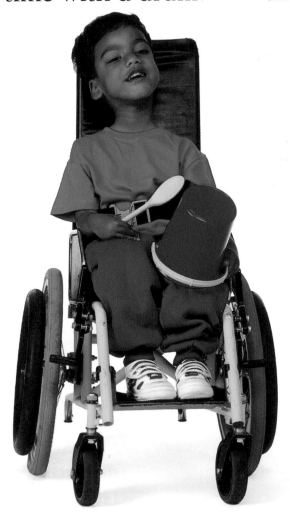

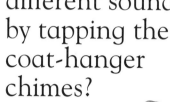

Beaters

Can you find a beater that makes a soft sound? Try making one by fixing elastic bands or cotton wool to the end of a pencil or knitting needle.

Shakers

Put some paper-clips or pasta into a plastic cup. Tape the cup to another cup to make a shaker. Can you shake it softly?

Coat-hanger chimes

Can you make lots of different sounds by tapping the coat-hanger chimes?

Box guitar

Can you make high and low sounds with the box guitar?

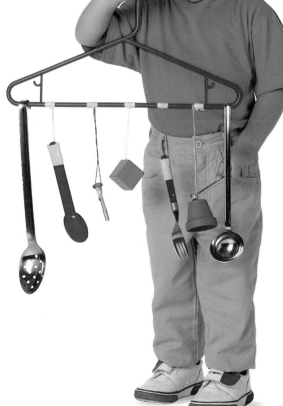

Index

Guide to experiments

The notes below briefly outline the scientific principles underlying the experiments and include suggestions for alternative equipment to use and activities to try.

Can you make sounds? 10-11

Here children use their bodies to make sounds. They use their voices, for example, when they sing, shout, or hum, and other parts of their bodies, for instance, when they clap or stamp. When they listen to a friend shouting, children will realize that loud sounds can be unpleasant. If children make a loud noise near a wall, they may hear sound reflected back to them as an echo.

Can you twang, pluck, or flap it? 12-13

Children cause objects or different materials to vibrate by twanging, plucking, or flapping them. Try varying the length or tension of the elastic bands. This will make the bands vibrate at a different speed when they are plucked and alter the pitch of the sound. As well as elastic bands, children could try plucking a loop of string.

28

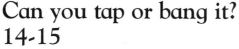

Can you tap or bang it? 14-15

When beating different objects, children will find that the quality of the sound produced depends on the material they are beating and the way they beat it. Ask children to tap hard and then gently so that they understand that the volume of a sound can be controlled. Let children find out what happens to a sound if the beaters are wrapped in cloth.

Can you shake or scrape it? 16-17

Making shakers and finding objects to scrape challenges children to experiment with different materials in order to achieve a desired sound. Children could also be asked to scrape corrugated cardboard with their fingernails.

Can you blow it? 18-19

These activities demonstrate that sounds can be produced by making air vibrate. By varying the length of a column of air, for example, by cutting the reed-pipe in half, children produce notes of different pitch. Asking children to blow hard and then gently reinforces the idea that the volume of a sound can be controlled.

Is the sound loud or soft? 20-21

Listening to soft sounds and making loud sounds reinforces children's understanding of the volume of a sound. By preventing sound from entering their ears, children develop the idea that ears are used for hearing and that sound travels through some materials, but not others.

Can you hear through things? 22-23

Here children are invited to investigate vibrations travelling through objects. Ask children to say which objects are good at carrying sounds. Try changing the length of the string in the string telephone, or changing it to nylon fishing line. Then ask children if they can hear better.

Can you feel it moving? 24-25

These activities enable children to detect vibrations. As well as using their fingers to detect vibrations, children could use other sensitive parts of their bodies, for example, their lips. Instead of a triangle, try the table-tennis ball held against a tuning fork.

Can you make music? 26-27

Here children are encouraged to use their instruments to make or accompany music. Let them decide which instruments and which rhythm to use and how the music will be structured. Children could also record their music on tape and then try to recognize their individual contributions.

29

PRINTED IN BELGIUM BY
proost
INTERNATIONAL BOOK PRODUCTION